TARGET
YOUR
ENERGY

TEXTBOOK

– A Book About Personal Effectiveness –
by Ingeborg Stemme and Lars Wiberg

Edited by Donna Rex.
Translated from Swedish by Susan Mogensen.

Printed in Sweden. Arne Svenssons Offset 1983.
ISBN No 91-7260-967-2.

In 1978, Lars Wiberg, a well-known author and management consultant in Sweden, was asked to produce a formalized "process of change" for the employees of Sweden's huge telecommunications company, L.M. Ericsson. The objective of this process was to help the individuals in the company to become more effective.

The program came on the market one year later. Since then almost 25,000 people have participated in this process of change in all kinds of organizations throughout Scandinavia.

Working with this program, Lars Wiberg found that success is measurable.

Ingeborg Stemme, a renowned specialist in measuring behavioral change, has conducted extensive research on the results of this program. Her evaluation has involved more than 1,200 participants – and her conclusions show that 70–80% of them have changed their personal working habits in a positive direction. The overall result was a higher level of performance with less stress.

Ingeborg Stemme co-authored Target Your Energy, and has also been instrumental in rewriting the program for the American market.

CHAPTER 1

WHAT DOES PERSONAL EFFECTIVENESS MEAN?

GOALS AND ENERGY MANAGEMENT.

Effectiveness means achieving your goals. Effectiveness means using your assets so they are not wasted. Effectiveness consists of both setting goals and managing your assets to achieve them.

When we use the term Personal Effectiveness, we are only talking about Personal Goals and the most important asset you have to achieve them – your own energy. So Personal Effectiveness means setting goals for yourself and managing your energy to achieve them.

Most adults lead two, parallel lives: a working life and a private life. Most of the illustrations we use are taken from working life, but the ideas are universally applicable.

No one lives in a vacuum, completely isolated from other people. If your Personal Effectiveness is low, it will affect other people around you, both at work and at home. If you apply the principles presented here, you will improve your Personal Effectiveness. At the same time that it makes life better for you personally, it will also contribute toward making life more effective for people around you. If you work more effectively, you help the organization that employs you to become more effective too. Not only because you are doing a better job yourself, but also because you are creating conditions that make it easier for your colleagues and associates to do a better job.

You probably learned many of your behavior patterns by copying others: parents, teachers, colleagues and bosses. When you work effectively, you in turn become a good role model for your colleagues and your own children to copy. This is an important form of influence.

JUNG OR FREUD? A QUESTION OF IDENTITY.

Freud, the father of psychoanalysis, developed new theories that have since come to influence the way people look at themselves. No one is a cut-and-dried entity, created whole. Everyone develops into what they are as adults based on their past experience. To a large extent, everyone is a product of her or his history.

On the other hand, Jung, another great psychologist, said: "Man can be fully understood only in relation to his goals." Jung meant that man is a product, not of his own history, but of the future he has chosen for himself.

At one time or another, you have probably asked yourself, "Who am I?" You can choose to answer that question according to either Freud's definition or Jung's.

If you choose Freud, then you look for reasons. You investigate your history and search for explanations. If you choose Jung, then you search for the meaning, the purposes and the goals.

Freud's reason-identity and Jung's purpose-identity are recurring themes in this book. We talk about the "must-world," based on Freud's definition, and the "will-world," based on Jung's.

A major problem for many people is that they are stuck in the "must-world." Life would be much easier and they could work more effectively and creatively if they could free themselves from the "must-world" and learn to live in the "live-world." In that respect, at least, we side with Jung. We think it is an exciting journey to take yourself out of the "must-world" and into the "will-world." It is exciting and demanding, but not dangerous.

Different worlds, different realities. Let us begin by looking at what reality actually is.

REALITIES.

The earth is round and turns on its own axis, even if some people believe it is flat and stands still at the center of the universe. The physical reality is what it is, regardless of what ideas people may have about it.

When it comes to social reality, though, the reality made up of people who interact, there is a big difference. People are not what they seem, regardless of what you think of them, or of yourself. You are influenced by your perceptions, and your perceptions influence others. Strictly speaking, your perceptions of reality are the only reality that exists. And you can influence and choose your perceptions.

THEORY X AND THEORY Y.

In his book, The Human Side of Enterprise, Douglas McGregor wrote that when people create organizations, with everything that entails in planning and control systems, they usually start with the expectation that employees are lazy and incapable of taking responsibility for their work. When people create organizations for lazy and irresponsible employees, those employees will confirm that expectation and behave lazily and irresponsibly. That is Theory X.

If, instead, people start out believing that employees are industrious and willing to take responsibility, they will create organizations for such employees, who will in turn confirm that expectation through their actions. That is Theory Y.

One company manager said, "If you treat adults like adults, then they tend to act like adults." And a successful teacher said, "Remember that if you take responsibility away from people, you create irresponsible people." These two advocates of Theory Y can say that their perceptions of people are confirmed by reality; that is, their experience of reality.

TWO CONCEPTS OF REALITY.

In this book, we have differentiated between two prime concepts of reality: the "must-world" and the "will-world."

THE "MUST-WORLD." In the "must-world," you must. You must do your job. You must look after your children. You must answer the telephone, you must go in to your boss when he asks for you. A variation on this theme is "I can't." I can't do it that way, I can't stop smoking, I can't... In the "must-world" your actions are determined by external impulses or by unchangeable qualities or ways of reacting within yourself. These make up the reasons why you act the way you do. "I can't stop smoking because I have such a weak character." "I can't ever remember people's names because I have such a bad memory." "I am this way and I can't do anything about it."

The "must-world" is governed by reasons that you may regard as fixed by law. Reasons push you from behind. There are seldom any alternatives in the "must-world," and there is always an explanation as to why you behave the way you do. In the "must-world" you can always justify yourself by referring to reasons. "It's true that things went wrong, but the reason I acted the way I did was..., and so it's not my fault that it didn't work out."

THE "WILL-WORLD." In the "will-world" you act according to your own will, you choose. You know that there are always different alternatives to choose from, even if none of them are particularly desirable. Often there is one alternative that is obviously so much better than the others that you hardly regard it as a choice. Sometimes there is no desirable alternative, but among the options available there is probably one that is less disadvantageous than the others, and you can choose that option.

The "will-world" is governed by purposes, which should attract you like a magnet, as opposed to the reason-determined "must-world," where you feel as if you are being pushed from behind. Purposes come from within you and are directed toward goals outside yourself. If you reach the goal, it is a consequence of your actions. So in the "will-world" you are more interested in the results of your actions than in the reasons behind them.

In the "will-world" you look at faults and mistakes as the results of your actions, and therefore of your own choosing. "It went wrong because I chose to act the way I did." You may be angry, unhappy, disappointed or irritated by the mistake, but you do not defend yourself by referring to reasons.

If you examine why things went wrong, you probably look for what was wrong in your own choice of action first, instead of what was wrong with everything else. This approach is a good way to accept responsibility and is also the best basis for finding new solutions.

ENERGY MANAGEMENT.

The "must-world" generates "must-energy." You recognize it as stress – sometimes it speeds you up and you can clear a lot off your hands. But sometimes it is paralyzing and you become unable to act. When using "must-energy" you may often act impulsively, allowing your reflexes to decide what you should do, as if you were acting according to a program. This probably leads to your automatically saying yes to things that afterwards you see you should have said no to. Or you may say no to something you ought to have said yes to. This automatic way of acting that produces undesired consequences belongs to what we call self-sabotage. It is you yourself who is sabotaging your intended goals.

On the other hand, the "will-world" generates "will-energy." You recognize it because it is focused on goals, with the purposes of your actions being well considered. When you try to solve a problem or achieve a purpose, you often find that things do not work out quite as you had expected. You then regard your actions as experiments, as a way of feeling your way toward your goal. So you learn by your mistakes and make a new attempt. If your purposes are clear and your goals realistic, then you will succeed.

Managing your energy is a dual problem. Partly, of course, it is a matter of influencing the flow of energy quantitatively. That is, how much energy do you have access to? And partly, it is a matter of learning how you can gain access to the qualitatively superior "will-energy."

You need, then: first, to learn how to take yourself out of the "must-world" when you have become stuck in it, and second, to learn how to identify and choose among the alternatives that are available in the "will-world." Energy management then becomes the switch between "must-energy" and "will-energy."

GOAL ORIENTATION.

Goals motivate you to act. If the goals are desirable and challenging, they generate a lot of "will-energy." But if you are to succeed in achieving your purposes, your goals must also be so clear that you can use them as a beacon to find the right path and identify alternatives.

Goals, all goals, should be clear and challenging to help you remain in the "will-world." But goals can also be in conflict with each other – you can only reach one at the cost of another.

That is when you need to learn to set priorities, to choose which goal is most important, and which ones are less important.

TO SUMMARIZE.

Personal Effectiveness means setting goals and managing your energy to achieve them.

To improve your Personal Effectiveness, you need to learn how to switch between "must-energy" and how to make your goals work for you.

CHAPTER 2

SELF-SABOTAGE IN THE "MUST-WORLD"

Self-sabotage is "an unconsidered action with undesired consequences."

You commit self-sabotage when you say yes to things that you should have refused. You commit self-sabotage when you say no to something that you should have agreed to, and when you escape from situations where you should have stayed put.

You put off jobs at work that you should do immediately, you say things you should not say or refrain from talking about something you should talk about because it feels unpleasant to say anything just then. Most people certainly have no shortage of self-sabotage acts, those unconsidered actions with undesired consequences.

Most often self-sabotage only affects you personally, but all too often it affects other people as well. Here are a couple of examples that illustrate, first, how you can be affected personally, and then how others can suffer as a result of your self-sabotage:

Barbara works in an office. One day she decided to use her lunch hour partly to buy a present for a good friend who was having a birthday and partly to prepare for a meeting that afternoon by reading over a memo.

Just as she was about to leave for lunch, a colleague came in and said, "Barbara, I need to talk with you during lunch hour, can we eat together?" Barbara could not say no, she felt she "must" help out. She did not buy the present and had to go to the meeting unprepared. Her act of self-sabotage mainly affected her personally.

Most people want to be considerate toward their fellow men. However, the following example shows how people can sabotage that intention and instead act in a way that can most accurately be described as brutal toward the very person they had really wanted to be considerate to:

Certain male managers carry their managership like an aura around them. They walk leaning slightly forward and take long strides, speak forcefully and have permanently clenched jaws. The Production Manager was just such a "real manager."

A lot of things happened during the 70s. Aside from the changes in planning and production technology, many changes were instituted in the Swedish legislature in the area of labor relations. There were new laws regarding holidays and education, and laws that strictly controlled the conditions regarding how employers were allowed to change their employees' work requirements.

The Production Manager could not adapt to all these new ideas. He was getting on in years and he thought everything had been better before the changes. There were many indications that his department was not developing very successfully: he had numerous conflicts with his staff, and he had difficulty in keeping to delivery commitments and his budget.

The company's top management met with the Production Manager several times. But it was unpleasant for them to criticize, especially so because the man was a senior staff member who had made great contributions to the company over many years. They spoke to him carefully about the problems, but did not make themselves sufficiently clear to him how the problems looked from their perspective. As a result, the Production Manager did not understand how seriously they viewed the problems and his part in the whole picture.

When the Production Manager was 58 years old, he

suffered from high blood pressure and had had a minor heart attack. The situation in his department at that time was completely untenable and something had to be done to avoid a catastrophe. But what could be done? Of course, the Production Manager was aware that the problems existed, but he felt they were due to the fact that the younger engineers did not do their jobs properly; people did not want to work, they only wanted to have holidays, and youngsters did not learn proper manners in school nowadays. He was also completely convinced that top management shared his opinion.

The company's top management contacted us and asked, "What should we do? We must move him, but if we do that, we risk his having another heart attack and dying." Because of their unconsidered way of handling the previous meetings with the Production Manager, they had put themselves in a position where, to solve problems in the organization, they must treat an old staff member in a way that he and many around him would consider brutal. Top management's self-sabotage in this case affected a person who could have had a considerably better and more worthy end to his career than he now received.

THE BACKGROUND OF SELF-SABOTAGE.

Self-sabotage is an action, and like all other actions it is founded on human needs.

You only notice your needs when they are not satisfied. You notice the need for food only when you are hungry, the need for heat when you are cold. You do not feel needs that are satisfied.

When your needs make themselves known, you can deal with them either by considered or by unconsidered actions.

CONSIDERED ACTIONS. When the need for company makes itself felt, you notice it in the form that you feel lonely. Loneliness is "cured" by contact with other people, so if you handle the need for company in a considered way, you decide whom you want to make contact with and in what way. If the attempt fails, you try again, maybe with the same person, maybe with someone else.

A considered action is aimed at an objective: the unsatisfied need should be satisfied. You focus on the result of your actions and choose among different possible alternatives.

UNCONSIDERED ACTIONS. Unconsidered actions could be called reflexes. According to the dictionary, a reflex is "an automatic response to a stimulus not involving higher mental centers."

The unsatisfied need often produces a feeling of craving: a craving to eat, a craving to sleep, etc. Other people's demands on you can also awaken such feelings of dissatisfaction – which clamor for immediate attention. That is the "Must-World."

The releasing mechanism for such unconsidered actions is either an attempt to get away from the immediate demand or an attempt to avoid getting into a demanding situation.

Unconsidered actions are, therefore, essentially a way of avoiding certain feelings or situations that coincide with the unsatisfied needs.

THREE PATTERNS
FOR UNCONSIDERED ACTIONS.

We have identified three different main patterns for a person's unconsidered and involuntary way of handling situations and feelings that, over and above the fact that the person experiences them as demands, also actualize the satisfaction of that person's needs:

The Yes-Reflex, which makes a person give in to whoever is making the demands.

The No-Reflex, which makes a person repel or keep out whoever is making the demands.

The Escape-Reflex, which makes a person try to get away from the demands or whoever is making the demands.

All three of these unconsidered ways of acting lead to self-sabotage if the consequences are undesired. If the consequences are desired, it is more a matter of luck; the result was not due to a conscious decision, but to a reflex.

Why do people act this way when the result is often in conflict with what they want? Why did Barbara say yes to a colleague? Why did the company's top management avoid a confrontation with the Production Manager at an early stage, a confrontation that could have helped him have a different view of the problems? The answer is that people act impulsively in an unconsidered way because in the short term it relieves them of the burden of experiencing an unsatisfied demand.

Because most people do not give themselves enough time to think through what it is they really want to achieve, neither do they have anything to balance against the unreflected action. Barbara could have considered accepting her colleague's invitation to lunch because she thought it more important to keep in contact with him than to do what she had previously thought of. But that is something rather different from her giving in without a thought to the consequences.

In the short term, these three reflex actions help people avoid feelings and situations that are connected with unsatisfied needs. Instead they help achieve something else that is more desirable:

REFLEX	AVOIDS	ACHIEVES
Yes, to give in	being expelled	being pleasing
No, to repel	being "invaded"	control of territory
Escape, to get away from	being a failure	lack of demand/ peace and quiet "oblivion"

To our way of thinking, these three reflexes are defense mechanisms. People defend themselves against being expelled, being "invaded" and/or being a failure, all of which they want to avoid. Behind these avoiding-goals, however, are what we call "true needs."

The need to avoid being expelled corresponds to the true need for Fellowship.

The need to avoid being invaded corresponds to the true need for Freedom.

The need to avoid being a failure corresponds to the true need for being a Success.

These three true needs are all very constructive. The need for Fellowship is an important foundation if people are to build societies and organizations. Freedom is important if people are to know vitality and the joy of life, so they can feel motivation. The need for Success is naturally an important driving force in all forms of development.

The opposite of fellowship is expulsion. The opposite of freedom is invasion. The opposite of success is failure. A person commits self-sabotage when, instead of trying to satisfy the true needs in a considered way, s/he instead acts in an unconsidered way as a means of avoiding the opposite of those true needs. A person commits self-sabotage when it becomes more important to avoid being expelled, thereby giving in to demands and trying to please, than to achieve fellowship on acceptable terms to both parties. A person commits self-sabotage when the need for freedom becomes a one-sided defense of her or his own territory instead of asserting a true freedom to try for meaningful goals, or when fear of failure prevents her or him from taking risks that are necessary for true success.

ROLES, TERRITORY AND INVASION.

Most people will probably recognize the Yes-Reflex' attempts to please and the Escape-Reflex' attempts to get away from a situation. The No-Reflex' attempts to control territory and to avoid invasion are harder to understand, so we will expand on them:

Animals have territories. Most wild animals, those on the African savannahs, for example, have three distinct territorial boundaries. As long as you keep outside the furthermost boundary, nothing happens. But if you cross that invisible line, the animal becomes alert and watchful. If you come closer and cross the second boundary, the animal will run away. But if you encroach on the innermost boundary, the animal will attack in self-defense. The animal's territorial boundaries are geographical.

Even people have geographical territorial boundaries in different situations. If you are driving a car and someone passes you then cuts into the lane directly in front of you, you will probably become disturbed or even angry.

But people have other ideas of territory as well. It is a good thing to have eye-to-eye contact with another person, but if you look for too long a period of time, you are staring. That is also a kind of territorial feeling. Contact, certainly, but not too intensive.

Most people play roles in many contexts. The Production Manager in the earlier example presumably played the role of being a "real manager." Roles often come in pairs. The authoritative boss comes in a pair with submissive staff members, the initiative-taking boss comes in a pair with employees who are lacking in initiative, etc. In order to succeed, one role must be complemented by another. Role play belongs in a pretty static environment, in a "must-world."

When one person wants to play a role and another person does not, the first person considers it an invasion of territory. Here is an example:

We were supposed to meet a manager, together with some of his associates. We were to meet in the manager's office, but when we got there he had not yet arrived. In the room were two sofas and between them was a chair, which was higher than the sofas. One of us sat on the chair.

After a couple of minutes, the manager came in. We greeted him and gestured for him to be seated on the unoccupied sofa. The manager said, "No, you sit there instead, it's more comfortable." The person sitting on the chair answered, "Thanks, I'm fine here." Then the manager said, "As long as we're going to work, we'll be better off in the conference room," and without waiting for an answer he stalked out of his office and led the group to the conference room. There he sat in the "chairman's" seat on the table's short side. The person who had taken "his" chair in his office had invaded the manager's territory, so he went off to another place where he could have control over territorial boundaries.

The manager who sees his role as being solely responsible for initiatives can construe it as trespassing onto his territory if associates come with suggestions for improvement. The No-Reflex often expresses itself as an unwillingness to listen to other people, an unwillingness to understand other people's points of view.

THE LINK BETWEEN SELF-SABOTAGE AND
THE DIFFERENT REFLEXES.

Sometimes it is easy to see if an act of self-sabotage is

caused by a Yes-Reflex or an Escape-Reflex. It can be more difficult in other situations. Did Barbara say yes to her colleague in order to give in to the demand or because she actually thought it would be boring to read the memo over lunch and was therefore willing to accept her colleague's invitation to lunch as an excuse to get out of reading it?

We do not know what the facts of the matter were with any certainty. But neither is it so important in regard to our aim with this book. We want to contribute toward a reduction in the number of acts of self-sabotage and thereby contribute toward better Personal Effectiveness. For this purpose, it is enough to know that self-sabotage is the result of unconsidered actions, but we do not believe that it is important to be able to classify the unconsidered action as a Yes-, No-, or Escape-Reflex in each situation.

TO SUMMARIZE.

In Figure 1 we have tried to summarize graphically what we have talked about in this chapter. Needs make themselves known as a feeling of dissatisfaction. This dissatisfaction gives rise to an action that can be a considered one, and if so, people choose from the different alternatives, evaluating them with regard to the possible consequences. You either succeed and enjoy success, or you fail and have to try again.

An unconsidered action is aimed at avoiding something, a feeling of dissatisfaction or the situation as such. An unconsidered action happens in the form of a reflex and can lead to undesired consequences that we call self-sabotage – or to desired consequences if you are lucky.

Success and failure go together with considered actions, luck and self-sabotage go together with unconsidered, reflex actions.

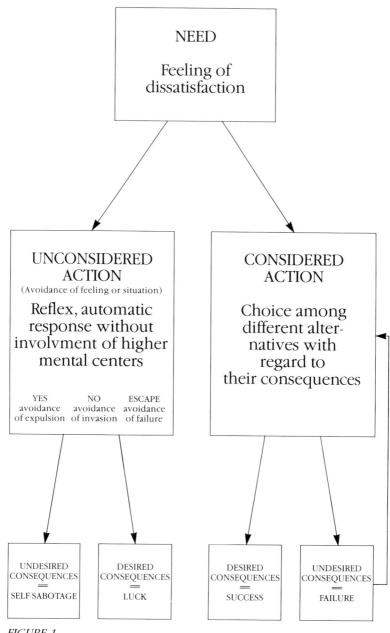

FIGURE 1

THE "TO-DO LIST" –
A TOOL TO COUNTER SELF-SABOTAGE.

Many, perhaps most, of people's acts of self-sabotage are a result of their using their energy for the wrong purposes. They are enticed into using their powers for short-term goals at the cost of the more long-term ones, or in order to get away from momentary demands and disturbances. It would be better if, instead, they could aim at carrying out planned activities or had time available for really important purposes.

In order not to be enticed in this way – and then be smitten by the sickly pallor of afterthought – you need to have a reasonably clear idea of what you actually have on your program, which commitments you must uphold, which time deadlines you must meet, etc. Then you can judge what can be fitted into your time and energy structures, you can make changes in a flexible way, within the structure of your commitments, without running into self-sabotage. Having a reasonably clear idea does not mean that you must work with a sophisticated time-planning system. On the contrary, then you would run the risk of being caught up in a new line of "musts."

The tool we would like to recommend is a calendar that, in a simple form, integrates days and times with fixed, planned commitments. The calendar makes it possible to catch in flight and fix onto paper everything that can become a commitment. So our "To-Do List" covers everything that you have definitely decided to do and when you will do it, but "when" is elastic; it can be a specific hour, a specific day or a specific week. The "To-Do List's" overview gives you the chance to orient yourself as to how much time you have available so you can use the gaps in a meaningful way. But above all, your "To-Do List" will prevent you from taking on unconsidered commitments for which there is no room in your program.

CHAPTER 3

SUCCESS IN THE "WILL-WORLD"

SUCCESS IS REACHING GOALS.

You are successful when you reach your goals. But being successful is not the same thing as being good. You are good when you do what other people expect you to do, when you are as other people think you ought to be.

Of course, you can be both successful and good. That happens when other people's expectations coincide with your own goals. But sometimes other people's expectations conflict with your goals, and then you have to choose between being successful and being good.

Here are a couple of examples:

Roger was the only son of a successful company owner. When we met him he was active in the family business, and it was taken for granted that he would take over after his father. But Roger was also musical, and really wanted to make a career as a songwriter and composer. There is a risk that he will "only" be good if he stays in the company, but he could be successful in the entertainment world.

Sometimes the choice between being good and being successful is not so clearcut. Elizabeth was a "General Solution" secretary. By that we mean she was one of those people who seem able to handle an unlimited amount of work, who always say yes to any and all assignments and take care of everything by themselves. Secretaries are frequently General Solutions, but this type of person can be found in many other occupations as well.

Elizabeth worked for a small but growing company.

After the first couple of years her boss decided that the workload required another secretary. However, after thinking it over, she decided that instead of taking on a new employee, she would give Elizabeth her own budget to buy the extra services from temporary clerical agencies. At the end of the year the boss found that none of the money had been spent! Instead of delegating the work to others, Elizabeth had stretched herself even more and done everything unassisted, not because she did not need the extra help but because of her inability to delegate.

People like Elizabeth are often promoted based on their capacity to work. But being an effective boss is very different from being a General Solution. An effective boss knows how to delegate, how to give support to subordinates, and how to raise productivity by involving others – not by doing everything by herself or himself.

We have seen General Solution bosses in auditing firms, R&D departments, banks and data processing companies. They take care of all the difficult and important jobs themselves. But by doing so they prohibit their subordinates from growing professionally by handling difficult work independently. General Solution bosses usually have an enormous workload and very brief and infrequent contacts with their subordinates – and they are not very effective bosses.

Depending on what your goal is, a General Solution pattern of behavior can either help you or hurt you. If your goal is to be the shining star of the department, then it is probably a successful strategy to deny anyone else the opportunity to shine. On the other hand, if your goal is to be an effective boss who helps your subordinates grow by motivating them and coordinating their work efforts toward common goals, then a General Solution approach will be detrimental to your efforts.

We have used these examples to underline that success consists of achieving the goals you want to achieve.

CONDITIONS FOR SUCCESS.

TO HAVE GOALS. To succeed in achieving your goal, obviously one condition for that success is that you in fact have a goal. Unfortunately, though, that is also a condition for failure. Only someone who has a goal can fail.

The following illustrations show that you cannot fail if you do not have a goal:

When Alice in Wonderland met the Cheshire Cat, she asked him:

"Which way should I go?"

"That depends on where you want to go," answered the Cat.

"I don't know," said Alice.

"Then it doesn't matter which way you choose," said the Cat.

And one of our thinkers in the field of marketing said: "If you don't know where you're going, any road will take you there."

Finally, we are great believers in this profound statement: "He who doesn't know where he is going will presumably arrive somewhere else."

Should we have clear goals?

On the surface, that is an easy question to answer. Each and every one of us certainly wants to be successful. But unfortunately it is more complicated than that. In the "will-world" you determine things yourself with the help of your purposes. In the "must-world" you are pushed forward by reasons, for example by the expectations of the people around you.

Living up to other people's expectations is important, of course. And you can do it without any problem if your goals are not in conflict with these expectations. Many people are afraid of making it clear to themselves what it is they want because they are afraid of finding out that it conflicts with what the people around them want.

And once you are aware of the conflict, you have to deal with it – either by trying to solve it, or by giving in to other people's demands at the cost of your own will, and that is never easy.

A person who lacks goals cannot fail. If failure is a serious threat, then any goals worthy of the name should be avoided at all costs. When we discussed escape reflexes earlier, we said they were aimed at avoiding failure. Some people choose a life strategy that avoids failure by avoiding clear goals.

Improved Personal Effectiveness requires a move from the "must-world" to the "will-world." The most difficult obstacle you will have to overcome to make this move is the shift to begin thinking in terms of goals – and not only because you are not used to it. More importantly, if you think in terms of goals, you will become aware of the risk of failure. And you will also uncover any conflicts that might exist between the demands of the people around you to be good and your own attempts to be successful. Then you will have to do something about it.

THE INITIAL POSITION.

The first condition for success is that you have a goal. The second condition is that you know where you are in relation to that goal. If you are in Boston, but firmly believe you are in Philadelphia, you will go wrong if you plot a route to New York, in spite of the fact that you are perfectly clear in your own mind about where you want to go.

Geographical illustrations are very clear, but may be a little difficult to apply to business life. Here is another example:

"In a recent psychological study when a random sample of male adults were asked to rank themselves on 'the ability to get along with others,' all subjects, 100%, put themselves in the top half of the population. Sixty percent ranked themselves in the top 10%, and a full 25% ever so humbly thought they were in the top 1% of the population." (T. Peters & R. Waterman, <u>In Search of Excellence</u>, Harper & Row, 1982.)

The conclusion we can draw from this and similar studies is that deep down most people think they are OK. This means that people look for confirmation of this conception from the other people around them. When they get confirmation, everything is in order. When they do not get it, they consider the people around them to be at fault.

Suppose this is the initial position when you want to influence other people: they are looking for confirmation that they are OK. Is this also your initial position when you go shopping, when you are a teacher, a boss, a salesman or a parent – is this the picture you have of your fellow human beings?

Some bosses, salesmen and parents succeed in their efforts to influence others. They have a good concept of their initial position, so they treat people from the perspective that they themselves think they are OK. Those who make negative criticisms, who moan or shout, only confirm to the people they are criticizing that it is the people around them who are at fault.

If you want to succeed, you need to be open to signals from others so that you can keep yourself informed about your present initial position. Then you can find ways to influence them in a positive manner.

In the "must-world" you shut out signals from others with the help of your no-reflexes, and you thereby fail to influence them because you do not know what your initial position is. You have too little understanding of your own ability, for example, or too little empathy to be able to appreciate other people's realities.

Here is another example to show that both conditions for success need to exist before you can succeed. That is, you need both to have a goal and to know your initial position in relation to it.

We have made similar studies in several companies and public organizations and found more or less the same problem in all of them. It looks like this:

Top management generally has a clear idea of the organization's goal. From middle management and downwards in the hierarchy, though, people only know how their business functions on a daily basis, what problems and opportunities there are. In other words, they know what their initial position is, what their reality is. But their picture of reality is not accessible to the people above them, which means that top management know where to go, but they do not know where they are in relation to the goal. Further down the hierarchy, people know what their initial position is, but are not clear about the goals, or even in which direction they are going. This tendency seems to be the same in many organizations.

We have two examples that show how effective it is to clarify ideas about your goal, where you are going, and where you are in relation to the goal so that the entire organization shares the same ideas. One example is IBM, where the Corporate Management Committee sees its most important task as keeping contact with the reality that exists in the organization, and communicating goals so that they are understood in the same way by everyone.

The other example is Scandinavian Airlines System, SAS. The president, Jan Carlzon, managed in a brief period of time to halt a downward development trend that was resulting in large losses and turn it around so that SAS made a good profit. He did it by understanding the company's initial position and by communicating a clear goal to everyone in the organization.

The goal that every SAS employee was supposed to focus on was to give support to the customer. Jan Carlzon made it very clear that regardless of whether you were selling tickets, serving coffee or handling baggage, you should focus on your customer's needs. If you did not have direct contact with the passengers, that did not change anything. You were supposed to define who your customer was and focus on her or his needs. The people who actually sold tickets, served coffee and handled baggage were the "customers" of the ADP Department, the catering service and the baggage handling supervisors, respectively.

Imagine the effect of this shift in focus: "I am not here to control my subordinates but to give them support so that they are able to perform at the peak of their abilities." Everyone can make this shift by asking themselves: "Who is my customer and what are that person's needs in her or his capacity as my customer?"

Here is another example of a more everyday variety:

In one medium-sized company the personnel's cafeteria did not function well. The food was bad, the tables were sticky, and morale among the cafeteria staff was very low. The managing director of the company spoke to the head of personnel, who was responsible for the cafeteria and who assured him that he had spoken to the staff, but that nothing helped.

The managing director himself got in touch with the cafeteria staff, who turned out to be completely ignorant of the fact that people were complaining. They felt they were stuck with moaning guests who did not contribute to making their work in the cafeteria particularly pleasant. It had not occurred to them that they could change the reality they lived in. Once they found out what their initial position was, they changed their attitude, and within a short time all the complaints had stopped.

But what about the head of personnel, the one who had first spoken to the cafeteria staff? Yes, he had talked to them, but it was an uncomfortable position for him. He was influenced by his need to please and to avoid discomfort when he criticized, so it is possible he did not make

himself clear. As we pointed out earlier, a "we're all win-
ners" attitude means people are looking for confirmation
that they are doing things right, and therefore they avoid
seeing their own mistakes. So if negative criticism is not
very clear, it is probable that it will not be perceived as
such.

This kind of fuzzy thinking is very common. You
have probably heard about the man who was going to be
fired, but who, when he came out of the meeting with his
boss, thought that he had been given a raise!

You need to understand what your goal is and where
your initial position is in relation to it before you can succeed.

POSSIBILITIES OUTSIDE THE "MUST-WORLD."

In the "will-world" you know what you want. You are in
contact with yourself because you are in contact with
your goals. In the "will-world" you know where you are,
you are in contact with others because of your ability to
see and listen to signals. In the "will-world" you have
enough distance from what you are doing so you can be
in contact with yourself and with people around you at
the same time. You have enough distance to see your initial position in relation to your goal.

The "must-world" exists only in your own imagin-
ation. The "must-world" is a structure that you create yourself, a structure that does not allow alternatives. Here are
some examples:

Tom was the leader for 25 managers at a training center outside Boston. One morning there were no newspapers. Tom asked the front desk staff several times if
there was any way they could get the newspapers. He was
told, yes, they would try, but there was something wrong
with the delivery van. In the end Tom called the local taxi
service and asked them to buy 25 newspapers and send
them in a car to the training center. The reception staff said
that was something you just could not do. The extra cost

for the newspapers was only $4, so why could it not be done? The answer is simple: There was no room for that solution within the structure of the desk staff's routines, within the boundaries of their "must-world." But there was certainly a solution outside their "must-world."

During a course in voice training, all the participants had to give a speech lasting between two and three minutes. When it was finally Bill's turn, all the other students had used between four and nine minutes. Bill asked his neighbor for help: "Time me, please. Hold up one finger after one minute, and two fingers after two minutes." Bill made his speech in two minutes and fifteen seconds and was complimented by the course instructor.

That made one of the participants furious. "He cheated, he cheated!" he shouted. "He had help to keep track of his time."

The assignment was to give a speech lasting about two to three minutes. Nothing was said about not using a watch, but in the fellow student's "must-world," that structure existed.

During training in practical learning methods for younger teachers, the participants had to carry out a lesson with "team teaching"; that is, two teachers taught the lesson parallel to each other. Many thought it was difficult. One said it was so hard to know what his colleague was thinking of doing next, that he felt uncertain. We pointed out that his colleague was actually in the same room with him, so he could ask her what she was thinking of doing next. That possibility did not exist in the young teacher's "must-world."

We often get one question from people who work with customer contacts: "How do I make contact with a customer?" You eat lunch together and as a salesman you want to establish deeper contact with your customer. What do you ask? Some people go through the whole list of hobbies, vacations, children, dog, etc. But once you have gone through this list, what do you ask then? We usually answer with a counter question: "What do you want to know?" Let that interest be the starting point and you will start a dynamic process that will go on as long as you like. Can you do that? Yes, but not if you believe there is a salesman's "must-world," complete with things you "must" and "must not" do or say.

When John discovered that he had lost his keys, he first looked for them in his pants pockets, then in his jacket pockets, then in his pants pockets, then in his jacket pockets, then in his pants.... The keys must exist. Yes, the keys do in fact exist, but not within the boundaries of the little "must-world" where John looked.

There is no "must-world" other than the one you create for yourself. You create it by looking for confirmation of your idea that there is a "must-world."

REWARDS IN THE "MUST-WORLD."

What advantages are there in living in the "must-world"? If the "must-world" does not exist and yet you live in it, then it must be tied up with some sort of advantage in living there.

The first advantage, or reward, is that it "feels" good in the "must-world." It feels like you get a lot done, and you get immediate relief from tension, worry and stress.

The other advantage is more serious: You free yourself from responsibility. In the "must-world," of course, it is always someone or something else that determines things. You yourself are innocent and free from responsibility. And responsibility can be a heavy burden to bear.

TO SUMMARIZE.

In the "will-world" there are always alternatives to choose from. In the short term there may only be a few alternatives. In the long term there are ususally several. The larger the piece of reality you include in your picture of the world, the more alternatives you can realize and the more obstacles you can get around.

Being able to choose what you want is not always the same as being able to choose what you desire. In the "will-world" there are always several alternatives to choose from, true. But there is no guarantee that any of the available alternatives are desirable.

You can only choose what is possible for you to choose. And when you choose, you must accept the consequences of your choice. Many people with low incomes may choose to be rich – but a consequence of that choice is strict economizing and doing without for many years. If you are not prepared to accept the consequences, you do not "want" to be rich, you only wish you were.

Many desires that are impossible to fulfill in the short term can be realized in the long term. Freedom of choice expands with a wider perspective. But not everything is possible even in the long term. You change a "want" to an expression of your will when you turn it into an action. You actively begin looking for possible ways to realize your will.

As we said earlier, one advantage with the "must-world" is that you do not have to be responsible for the consequences of your actions. In the "will-world" you are free to choose – and you are always aware that you will have to accept responsibility for what you choose. Responsibility is linked to free will. When you avoid taking responsibility, you also miss out on freedom. You cannot have one without the other.

CHAPTER 4

ENERGY MANAGEMENT

Energy management can be viewed from two perspectives: How much energy do you have access to? What kind of energy will you be able to tap into? The first (How much...?) we call the quantity aspect. The second (What kind...?) we call the quality aspect.

THE QUANTITY ASPECT.

Healthy people who eat well, get enough sleep, look after their constitution and abstain from alcohol and tobacco, have more energy than they would if they were sick, ate carelessly, slept less, did not get any physical exercise and used both alcohol and tobacco. What we are trying to say by this is that, to a certain extent, your energy level depends on the lifestyle you have chosen. This seems to be such an obvious fact that we will not dwell on the well-known connection between your energy supply and your way of life.

People were created with rhythms. You feel better because of the changes between tension and relaxation, between movement and rest, between work and leisure. If you deny your need for these kinds of natural rhythms over a long period of time, you wear yourself out – and that is not effective.

During the day you also have certain biological rhythms, which give you more energy at certain times than at others. The time of day when these energy-filled periods occur differs from one individual to another. You can find out what your own rhythms are and use this knowledge as a basis for deciding when to do different things.

Not all people have the same amount of energy. If people with a lot of energy use their own energy supply as a norm for the people around them, they risk wearing out their co-workers. That is not effective either.

We will leave the quantity aspect at that. It is certainly important, but for one thing, it has already been dealt with by numerous other writers, and for another, it is probably familiar to most people anyway.

THE QUALITY ASPECT.

Like most people, at some time or another you have probably worked under great pressure. There was a rush on, you were stressed, but worked quickly and became very irritated if you were disturbed.

And, like most people, at some time or another you have probably also concentrated on trying to find the solution to a problem. It could have been a difficult move in chess, a construction problem, the wording of a report, or how to saw the ceiling moldings so they would fit snugly when you redecorated your living room.

In both situations, when you work under pressure and when you concentrate on a problem, you have access to a lot of energy – but it is not the same kind of energy. When you work under pressure, you work quickly, are tense and often divided. When you solve problems, you concentrate, seek the solution slowly, and are often fairly relaxed.

We call these two types of energy "program-energy" and "will-energy," respectively. "Program-energy" can be found in abundance in the "must-world." "Will-energy" is only found in the "will-world."

"Program-energy" is fast and action oriented. When it is channeled into purposeful action patterns it can be very effective. But when it is channeled into action patterns that are not purposeful, it becomes destructive and can lead to self-sabotage. "Program-energy" is not creative. You can use it to choose quickly between some known possibilities, like John did when he looked for his keys in his pants-jacket-pants-jacket pockets. But you cannot use it to discover new possibilities.

"Will-energy" is slower. You can use it to find solutions and to create new and better possibilities. "Will-energy" is creative and goal oriented.

When you get stuck, when you do not succeed with what you have set in front of you, when you are on the wrong track, then you need "will-energy." But the fast, unconsidered and rigidly programmed "program-energy" is a great help in solving many small problems that appear in a similar fashion every time you encounter them. People who engage their "will" when all they are going to do is button buttons, tie a tie, or press the keys on a typewriter will soon find themselves worn to a frazzle.

Anyone who has two typewriters with some of the keys in different positions on the respective keyboards, notices that each time s/he changes machines, s/he has to change her or his "program".

S/he presses the wrong keys a few times, but fairly soon s/he has switched over to the conditioned reflexes for that specific machine. It is practical.

Energy management means learning how to gain access to the type of energy that best suits you at any particular moment. You can let your "will-energy" take care of the decisions, and then turn loose your "program-energy," the programmed behavior appropriate to the decisions you have just made. That is what you do when you play tennis, drive a car or ski. You decide of your own free will where you want to go, what your goal is, and then let your relexes take care of the work. Note that in this case these reflexes are different from those we earlier called "yes," "no" and "escape" reflexes. These reflexes should not be considered defense mechanisms.

ENERGY MANAGEMENT –
MOVING TO AND FROM THE "WILL-WORLD."

The most difficult part of managing energy is moving from "program-energy" to "will-energy." Engaging your program-guided reflexes within the limits of a consciously made decision is something you can learn fairly easily. It is not difficult to let the program take over the energy in this way. But to make the other move is much harder.

"Program-energy" confines you to a limited reality and you feel stress. To tap into "will-energy" you need to get away from the confinement and stress of the "must-world" – you need to get distance from yourself and the situation you are in.

The "ladder" that will help you move from the restrictions of "program-energy" to make contact with your "will-energy" instead has three rungs: Alternative, Distance and Goal.

ALTERNATIVE. There are no alternatives in the "must-world." If you make yourself aware that there are <u>always</u> alternatives, then you automatically eliminate the "must-world" altogether. At the same time, you get rid of the "dream-world" where you tie up your energy in vain wishes that everything could be different. You can make yourself aware of alternatives with the help of the following sentence:

"Which is my best available alternative right now?"

In the short term, in the limited reality, there may be few alternatives. In the more long term, broader reality there are sure to be several. You need a tool that will help you get a little distance from your situation, a tool that will make it possible for you to have a "helicopter perspective" so that reality will be bigger and richer in alternatives. Before we go into how you can get distance, though, we will take a closer look at what we call stress.

Pressure and Stress. Stress is a condition you probably recognize. In physiological terms, you are stressed when the adrenal cortex secretes adrenaline, which activates the sympathetic nervous system, which in turn leads to increased blood pressure, among other things. Stress also affects you mentally. When you become stressed, your creative ability is blocked, and also your ability to evaluate different actions. Stress makes you less discriminating and less imaginative.

You may often become stressed in pressured situations where you are subjected to a lot of external demands and expectations. Things become really bad when you are subjected to conflicting demands that you cannot handle. Stress is a way of reacting to the external pressure, and it is different for different people. So it is not the situation in itself that produces stress – it is the individual who reacts with more or less stress, depending on the situation and on how s/he is disposed toward stress.

How you react in different contexts depends partly on the external situation, and partly on your attitude toward what is happening. If you want to change your reaction, therefore, you can choose either to change the external events, or to change your own attitude toward them.

Here is a two-part example:

1. Alex, Jr. works at the reception desk in a hotel. One morning an irate guest came in and complained about the

service. He had several complaints and ended up by saying that he was going to write a letter to the hotel's board of directors telling them what an incompetent staff they had. Alex, Jr. felt both unhappy and angry. He tried to argue with the guest without success, and after the guest left, Alex felt upset for the rest of the day.

2. Let us take that again, only this time the irate guest confronted Alex, Sr. Their conversation sounded like this:

G: The service here is really terrible.

A: We sometimes have guest complain, and that's never pleasant. What seems to be the problem?

G: Last night it took 30 minutes to get a sandwich and a beer up to my room. This morning I had ordered breakfast for 7:30 and it didn't arrive until almost 7:45, and now I've been waiting 20 minutes to pay my bill.

A: (who knows the guest has not waited more than about five minutes) replies: I can understand that you're upset. We really do try to give good service here, and you must have had an unusually bad time. I'd like you to come back again so you can see for yourself that our service is normally very good. What can I do to compensae you for your trouble?

The outward situation in examples 1 and 2 was the same. But Alex, Jr.'s attitude caused him to react with stress, while Alex, Sr.'s attitude gave him no stress reaction. He acted using his "will-energy."

You probably react with stress in pressured situations, but you may also react in a similar way when the pressure is too low; when you have nothing to do, for example. Retirement, unemployment or other forms of enforced free time over a long period can sometimes cause reactions similar to those you experience when you have too much pressure from outside.

If you have been under pressure and stress over a long period, your body adjusts and becomes accustomed to functioning with a higher level of adrenaline. When you break away from this and enter a calm period, you may experience a type of uneasiness. The experience feels almost like an abstinence reaction. After a stressed week at work, you may feel depressed, apathetic or react with purely physical symptoms such as a headache or a sore throat when Saturday rolls around. The first week of a vacation can produce similar reactions. These "abstinence symptoms" disappear after a while, but the discomfort can be so hard to bear that you may try to get back into new pressure situations instead of waiting until the aftereffects of the stress have worn off. That is when you can run into self-sabotage because of your escape-reflex.

<u>Positive and Negative Stress.</u> Most of you know that stress is harmful to your health. It leads to high blood pressure, circulation disorders and other types of psychosomatic reactions and illnesses.

In recent years people have agreed that there is probably another form of stress that is not harmful to your health. It is sometimes called "dynamic tension," or positive stress, and is experienced as a stimulus.

The difference between positive and negative stress is, to a large extent, a question of how much control the individual perceives s/he has over her or his situation. Someone who feels compelled or obligated, who sees no way out, who is afraid of being punished, who is subject to conflicting demands that s/he cannot handle, suffers from negative stress. On the other hand, someone who is in control of her or his situation, who knows that there are different ways of managing problems, who is not afraid of being punished, who feels that although s/he has a lot to do s/he can manage, who feels that s/he is working for something meaningful, operates from positive stress.

Positive stress is not harmful to your health. That is important, of course, but in this book it is not your health but your Personal Effectiveness that is in focus. Positive stress can be just as detrimental to your effectiveness as negative stress. You can be working on, and be stimulated by, a way of solving a problem that does not lead toward your goal. That involvement can result in your giving that work higher priority at the cost of a more important job.

We have seen this type of behavior repeatedly among lecturers who work without a manuscript, among interviewers and among participants in group work in courses. A lecturer may be speaking when s/he suddenly thinks of an example. S/he tells the audience that example, which in turn feeds another, etc. After a while either s/he or someone from the audience realizes that the lecturer has completely lost the thread of the lecture. The same thing happens to an interviewer who associates with something the respondent says and starts to ask questions about the side subject instead of staying on course with the actual topic.

So from an effectiveness point of view, positive stress can be just as bad as negative stress.

We can describe stress in general from either a physiological or a psychological point of view. However, our focus is on effectiveness and from that perspective we would like to define stress as "inadequate tension in relation to the goal."

If tension is too high, you lose creativity and the distance needed to find appropriate alternatives. If tension is too low, you do not have enough energy to stay on track or to act. Actually, if the motivation for a goal is too low, it can have the same effect as if tension were too low in relation to the goal. When you feel challenged, you feel "adequate" tension.

DISTANCE. In the short term, most things are impossible. The more you widen your perspective, though, the more possibilities there are. In the limited "must-world" there are few if any alternatives. Outside these boundaries there are more. So you need to gain access to the broader reality, the "helicopter perspective." You accomplish this by getting distance.

Most people have experienced how effective distance is. Many bosses have said something like this: "You get paid for being at work, but the really good ideas, the solutions to difficult problems, don't occur to you during working hours. You get those at home." Sound familiar?

The French expression "esprit de l'escalier" exactly illustrates the value of distance. It loosely translates as the idea you get on the stairs, on the way home or after the debate, when you have got some distance from the situation.

Awareness of the fact that you re-evaluate situations once you have got some distance from them can sometimes be too much for some people. A very aggressive journalist who was very fond of debates once took part in a political discussion. He became so enraged with his opponent that he got up, stomped out of the room, slamming the door behind him. There was total silence in the room. Before the general hubbub had started up again, the door flew open and the still-furious debater stuck his head in and roared, "And remember, if I apologize tomorrow, I don't mean it!"

Humor, not trivial, malicious pleasure, but warm, acknowledging, understanding humor, is an expression of distance. As long as you can smile indulgently at your own shortcomings, you will not risk developing a complete intolerance for other people. An interest in other people – customers and colleagues, for example – is also an expression of distance. In order to be genuinely interested in others, though, you need to get outside yourself. Egocentric people cannot have much distance from themselves. Self-centeredness often causes a jam in the "must-world," where there is no distance. "Will-energy" has more distance than "program-energy."

Awareness. Awareness is an including phenome-
non. You are aware of…something. Awareness requires
distance so you can include both your goal and an understanding of your initial position at the same time.

Distance provides the basis for intellectual understanding – the clinical, analytical, objective way of understanding. But if you only have distance, it can lead to cyni-
cism: you understand, but do not care. Therefore,
distance needs to be balanced with the emotional understanding that we call contact.

To have contact means to feel. You understand how
others feel by understanding your own feelings. Contact
is a way of recreating someone else's experience of a situation within yourself.

Awareness is a dynamic mixture of distance and contact, of aloofness and closeness.

Distance and Personal Effectiveness. The cynic needs
contact and the stressed person in the "must-world" needs
distance. We will concentrate on the distance problem,
though, because that is much more common.

There are different ways to get distance. Some people
listen to music, others go to a movie. You can read or do
physical exercise, sleep for a while, or take a walk. Most
people have their favorite methods, which they more or
less consciously choose.

We would like to strike a blow for a particular form of
getting distance; namely, a relaxation technique. We do
not want anyone to stop using other methods that work
for them. We would just like to add another model that has
also been proven to work well.

Relaxation. If you are out walking and suddenly see a
rattlesnake on the path, or if you are lounging in your
favorite comfortable chair and someone drops a stack of
plates in the next room, you will feel an immediate reaction in your body. Things heat up, you become tense and
wide awake. Stress researchers call this the "fight-or-flight

response." It is a stress reaction.

In a similar way, you can recognize the "relaxation response," which is just the opposite of the stress reflex, when you move from tension to relaxation.

Our recommended relaxation technique is a simplified form of meditation. The objective is to take you out of yourself, out of the "must-world," so you can get a little distance.

In our version, you start by sitting or lying comfortably. If you are at work you can take a chair and place it close to a wall so you will have support for your head when you lean back.

The problem with the "must-world" is that your energy and attention are tied up in places where you do not want them to be. You are now going to move your attention to your own body instead, and thereby break out of your confinement in the "must-world."

When you are sitting as comfortably as possible, think about how it feels to sit. You can feel three pressure points: your feet against the floor; your buttocks against the chair seat; and your back against the back of the chair. If you have support for your head, then you have a fourth pressure point. Begin by comparing these different pressure points. They are your contact with the earth.

Now let your attention move to your left hand. Tighten the muscles in your hand and hold them rigid for a few seconds. Relax and feel the difference. That is relaxation – the absence of tension. Tighten once more and then relax your hand.

Next let your attention wander slowly up through your left forearm, past your elbow and up to your shoulder. Feel whether your shoulder is relaxed. If it is hard to feel contact with your muscles, move them slightly until you find them, and then try to relax them with the same technique you used on your hand.

Repeat this exercise for you right hand, arm and

shoulder. Now continue to go through all your muscle groups, one by one. Let your attention wander up to your face, down through your throat and neck, shoulders, arms, hands. Keep going down through the upper part of your body, along your spine, then around to your diaphragm, where you should stop and explore how it feels to breathe.

After that, continue down through your stomach, buttocks, along your thighs, past your knees and down behind your calves to your ankles and feet. Then turn around and "travel" back up again.

Many people find the "relaxation response" the very first time they try this exercie. Others have to make several attempts over a period of time.

We have recorded this relaxation exercise on an audio cassette so that with the help of a cassette recorder it is easy to carry out the exercise many times. It only takes about 15 minutes, but gives you so much new energy that most people find it a profitable way to use their time.

We have several reasons for strongly recommending that you work with this relaxation technique. Here are a few of them:

When you have learned how to find the "relaxation response," this functions as a distinct goal for relaxation and you do not use any more time than you need to get distance. So, by using the exercise, you have a clear picture of what to look for when you need distance. That goal is the "relaxation response." Most other methods for getting distance are more time-consuming. Besides which, there is a risk that people will use their need to relax as an excuse to escape from a situation where it would be more effective for them to stay and work things out. That risk hardly exists with this relaxation exercise.

Stress activates the sympathetic nervous system. Relaxation voluntarily decreases activity in the nerve fibers. In a way similar to all the other processes in your body, this is something you can train yourself to do. The better trained you are, the faster you get distance and the faster you can find a new plan of action. Good training is achieved by using this relaxation exercise regularly over a period of weeks. Once you have learned the technique, you will not need the cassette anymore. You can then get distance yourself whenever you need it.

A third reason why we recommend this relaxation technique is that it is still a foreign occurrence in working life – and it should not be. Regardless of your starting point, we know for a fact that the ability to get distance contributes to improved effectiveness. There is an abundance of research results and well-documented experience that supports this belief. In spite of this, it is difficult to convince the general populace that they should use this relaxation technique. In one of our courses, a participant reported that he had used the technique regularly over the latest two-week period, and he considered it very effective. Several times he had handled situations differently and better than he otherwise would have, thanks to the distance he had gained through the relaxation exercise.

But when we asked him if he intended to continue with the technique, he answered no. "As long as the course continues I can always use it as an excuse if anyone sees me," he said. "But what do I say afterwards if a colleague comes into my room and sees me? He'll ask if he woke me up!"

The more people who use the relaxation exercise, the faster the ineffective opposition to it will disappear. Therefore, we want to recommend strongly that everyone use the technique. It is easy, effective and free.

TO SUMMARIZE.

The ladder that will take you away from the restrictions of "program-energy" and put you in contact with "will-energy" has three rungs:

Alternative, which you can identify with the help of the question: "Which is my best available alternative right now?"

Distance, which you can get by using many different methods, but we would especially recommend your learning the relaxation technique described earlier.

Goal, which is such an important rung that we have given it two chapters of its own. As a starting point, a simplified way of identifying and setting goals is to use the following reasoning, which should be familiar to you by now:

"There are always alternatives. This means I can always choose, I can always accept responsibility for my choice, and I can act according to my own will."

But sometimes no desirable alternative exists among those available. You can then choose the one that is least disadvantageous, but that is not much comfort. You still have to act contrary to your own wishes.

As some kind of consolation, we can put forward another of our theses: In the short term, most things are impossible; in the long term, almost anything is possible. Even though everything may not be possible, if you can get a little distance and widen your perspective to include the long term, you will increase your chances of finding at least one desirable alternative. This leads to the question:

"What would I rather have instead?"

A man we know was complaining about life: "Every day it's the subway to work, shuffle around a lot of paper and talk to people between 8:00 and 5:00. Collect the kids from the daycare center. Dinner, TV and Goodnight. It's too restricting and monotonous."

We asked what these daily routines prevented him from doing, what would make his life more meaningful? He could not think of an answer just then. But a few days later he called and said that he had benefited from our question. "It's my own inability to decide what I want that makes life empty, not the fact that I go to the office five days a week," he said.

If you like, life can be pretty monotonous. You may think: "I sleep seven hours a night, am awake seventeen; I have a Monday, a Tuesday, a Wednesday, a Thursday, a Friday, a Saturday and a Sunday every week; I have a winter and a summer in their seasons; and a birthday on the same day every year. Life is pretty monotonous. And besides, a hundred years from now it won't matter what I do today, so it's meaningless as well."

Of course you are free to choose this attitude that makes life monotonous and meaningless. But there is an alternative, as we said: "What would I rather have instead?"

CHAPTER 5

GOAL
ORIENTATION

THE FREEDOM TO CHOOSE.

When you free yourself from the "must-world," you gain access to several alternative possibilities to choose from. You discover that you have the freedom to choose.

Freedom to choose from different alternatives is the only true freedom that exists. The dream of absolute freedom, where everything can be realized immediately without any negative consequences for anyone or anything, will never be anything other than a dream – and a pretty bad dream at that. A complete absence of opposition also means an absence of friction and tension. That is why it is so boring. It is restrictive, too, because you need friction in order to move. If the dream of absolute freedom were to come true, you might find that total freedom also means total lack of power. Under absolutely frictionless freedom, you would have to give up striving to decide for yourself where you want to go, and instead surrender yourself entirely to powers beyond you.

The freedom to have several available alternatives to choose from is very valuable. But even this freedom can be difficult to bear, and can lead to frustration. Which of the available alternatives should you choose? When you choose one, you probably discard the others – and what if later on one of them proves to be better? What happens if you make the wrong choice? How do you know which is right? When you know you have many possibilities, but lack the ability to do anything with them, you get a guilty conscience; you feel guilty about your inability to choose. You probably also feel guilty in advance for maybe making a mistake, choosing the wrong possibility.

Some people deal with their uncertainty by becoming greedy: they collect potential, without having any idea of what they are going to do with it. The potential can be money or other possessions, but it can also be information, power or meaningless knowledge.

We can illustrate how frustrating freedom can be with the following story:

Ken is a middle manager in a large company. As a child he sailed a lot and when he grew up he got his own boat as quickly as possible. He married, and his wife also liked to sail. After a few years, by the time they began to think of having a family, Ken and his wife had a very big sailboat.

When the children arrived, Ken and his wife felt they should have a large house to raise them in. So they bought a house, but one that was a bit too large to afford on the family's one existing income. However, they agreed they would just have to cut down on luxury items.

We now have a little family with a mother and father and two small children, a large house and a big sailboat – and one middle manager's income. What do you think they should do on their vacation?

The answer is obvious: they should go sailing, of course.

Last spring we met Ken again. He told us he had sold his sailboat for $33,000. We asked him what he intended to do with all the money, and he said he did not know. Now let us ask the same question again: What do you think they should do on their vacation? If you think they should go sailing again, fine, but where? Off New England, in the Gulf of Mexico, to the West Indies, along Baja California? They can sail almost anywhere for $33,000. Or they can also stay at home in their large house, which

Ken could not do when he had an expensive sailboat because of the guilt feelings that would have created.

The simplest solution to Ken's problem would be for him to buy a new sailboat. Then he would not have to choose. The simplest solution would be to get rid of the freedom, or to escape from it, and that is exactly what a lot of people do. We usually call this attitude "Escape from Freedom," and we do not think it is a very good alternative.

A more constructive way to handle freedom is to use it to achieve what you want. What do Ken and his family want from their vacation? What goals do they have in their life together? In order to handle freedom this way, you need to decide what your goals are. It is also a problem of choice, which in turn can give you cause for a new escape from freedom.

You need to have a goal to get away from the "must-world." Your alternative actions then have different values for you, depending on how they can contribute to helping you achieve your goal. An alternative that definitely leads toward your goal is worth choosing over one that does not lead toward it.

An alternative action that leads toward a more urgent goal is worth choosing over one that leads toward a less urgent goal. And the possibilities that do not lead toward any goal at all become so insignificant that you may not even see them.

THE GOAL'S VALUES.

A goal symbolizes something you want to attain, something you think has value. When you have achieved your goal, you have attained the desired value and no longer need the symbol. However, some values cannot be achieved once and for all. Among these are moral values such as freedom and justice. We call the value that a goal symbolizes the Result Value, since the goal is a symbol for the desired result.

We do not pay much attention to the goal's Result Value in this book. It is certainly important, but should be self-evident to most people.

From the point of view of effectiveness, which is our present perspective, the goal has other and less obvious values. The goal helps you find ways through, and stimulates you not to give up. The goal can function as a motor for the job at hand. We call such values Motivating Values.

MOTIVATION. Motivation is sometimes described as the "will to." The will to exert yourself, the will to attain, the will to do something. In order for you to have motivation, the "will to," certain requirements have to be fulfilled:

- You need to understand what your goal is, what you have to do to reach it.
- You need to want to see the goal achieved, want to have results.
- You need to believe in your ability to do what has to be done.

The goal's Motivating Values are stronger the clearer the connection is between the values and the actions that are going to lead to the goal. That is, if you understand your goal so well that you can clearly see how you should act, then your "will to" act is stronger than if the connection is unclear. If you see the connection between your goal's desirability and your actions, then you are more motivated than when you do not see "what's in it for me."

If you can see clearly how to act so that you will succeed, you have a stronger "will to" than if you are uncertain of your ability.

You can be strongly motivated even without the Motivating Values being based on rational or realistic connections between the goal and the actions that will lead to it. You can believe you have a clear understanding of what your goal looks like, but if your notion is incomplete or inaccurate, then your understanding of your goal will be insufficient or even misleading. To succeed, you need a clear picture of <u>what</u> the goal is and of <u>where</u> it is in relation to your initial position. In addition, you need to believe in your own ability to reach your goal, either by yourself or together with others.

At heart, Bob was a true engineer. In his car he had all kinds of technical devices, including a compass. Bob and a colleague were on a business trip together in his car. They were in a town not far from San Francisco, on their way to its main hotel. Bob started to turn right, but his colleague corrected him and said: "We're going to the hotel, we should turn left." "Oh, no," said Bob. "I always drive using the compass, so I never go wrong." "Well, this time you are wrong," said his colleague. "I used to live here when I was a kid, so I ought to know where the hotel in Burlingame is." "Burlingame," said Bob, surprised. "Aren't we in Palo Alto?"

Bob knew where they were going, he was clear about their goal. But he was not at all clear about where they were in relation to the goal, he was not clear regarding his present initial position. We dealt with this earlier, in Chapter 3, where we talked about the prerequisites for success.

You need to know what your initial position is and where the goal is if you want to succeed. Plus you also need to be able to carry out the required actions. These expectations are based on rational and realistic assessments of reality.

But if you only had such rational and realistic assessments to refer to, success would be pretty rare and actually not very exciting. You may often find yourself in situations where you have an intuitive but vague picture of your goal, or where you are not sure about your initial position. And sometimes you may be unclear about both at the same time. Sometimes you are faced with a new problem. This applies nearly every time a consultant meets a new client for the first time. It also applies when you meet with colleagues and customers over a new idea. What is the goal and what is your initial position? How do you know if you have the ability to solve the problem?

Luckily, you can compensate for these uncertainties. By trial and error you can find your way to more and more distinct goals. You can clarify where you are by being interested and asking questions, or by acting and being receptive to feedback. By testing and experimenting you can develop the ability you presently lack. If you really want something and strongly believe in your own ability, then you can apply yourself to a search process, even though the end result is unclear. Trial and error can guide you and intuition can lead you if you are open and able to respond to vague but important signals.

In unfamiliar territory you have to feel your way toward success. If you have previous experience with success, though, you have the confidence to try again. If it succeeded last time, it should work this time too.

Inventors and artists are often people who are driven by a strong desire to achieve goals that are not distinct. They feel their way toward their goal with the help of intuitive ideas. The Danish inventor and poet Piet Hein once said: "Art is the solution for problems that cannot be clearly formulated until they have already been solved." In that respect, there are many "inventors and artists" even in ordinary business life.

Naturally, not all jobs will inspire you with a strong "will to." Filling in budget forms and vacation schedules, itemizing expense accounts, and reorganizing your desk are undeniably tasks that are both understandable and desirable. You know you can handle them, but even so they do not generate a particularly strong "will to." There are two ways to deal with them:

If you have access to a lot of energy, then boring tasks get done "into the bargain." You always have a lot of energy for the jobs you really want to do. The boring jobs are in the way of the stimulating ones, and they can be done quickly with the energy you get from what you really want to do. Here is an example of what we mean:

Mary is in her last year of high school. Her great interest in life is playing the violin, and it is this interest that generates her energy, her "will to." Like most teenagers, Mary is only moderately interested in her schoolwork, but she knows that if her grades suffer they could threaten her freedom to play the violin. Mary has good grades, she does her schoolwork well – with violin energy.

The other way to handle boring tasks is to redefine your goal. The goal is not "to fill in an expense account form," but rather "to have filled in an expense account form." Working on the form itself is nothing to cheer about, but the relief of getting it over with is something that can give you the "will to."

DIRECT MOTIVATION FUNCTIONS AND GENERATIVE FUNCTIONS.

So far we have dealt with the direct connection between goals and motivation. The goal is a symbol for a desired condition and thereby symbolizes the value of that condition – the Result Value. If you understand your goal's Result Value, if you consider it desirable to attain, and if you believe in your own ability to do so, you will develop the "will to," or rather, motivation. So Understanding, Desirability and Credibility are values that must be directly connected to your goal in order for your goal to help you develop motivation or a "will to."

In addition to these Direct Motivation Functions, goals, particularly the more complex ones, have yet another level of Motivating Functions. We call them the goal's Generative Functions. Along the way these functions generate Motivating Values that have a further and more comprehensive influence on your motivation in an extended development context. These values, which we call Development Values, are less directly connected to the goal than the Specific Goal Values that we have talked about thus far; namely, Understanding, Desirability and Credibility.

Figure 1 illustrates the connections between the terms we have been discussing so far:

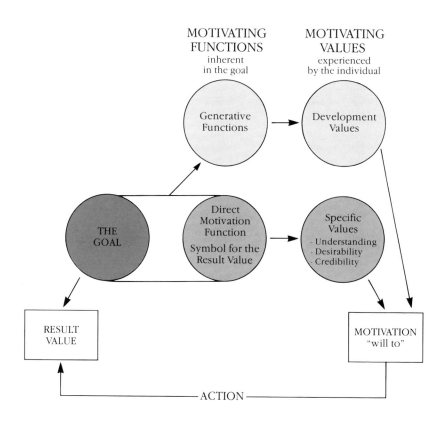

FIGURE 1

THE GOAL'S GENERATIVE FUNCTIONS.

The goal has three Generative Functions:

– The Detector Function
– The Generator Function
– The Development Function

THE DETECTOR FUNCTION. We will start with a three-part anecdote to illustrate what we mean:

1. Every person we have asked about it has answered, "Sure, I have a box like that at home." This box is where you put left-over pieces and other odds and ends. For example, after having bought a new bookshelf and assembling it according to the instructions, you find you have a piece left over, a piece you do not need. In the box are not only pieces left over from bookshelves, but also screws and nuts, fittings for curtain rods, plastic lids, copper wires, pieces of tape and string, etc.

2. Sam was going to vacuum the house one Sunday afternoon, but the vacuum cleaner would not work. Sam took out a screwdriver, dismantled the machine, and soon found which piece was causing the problem. He needed a spare part, but it was Sunday and of course the hardware store was closed. What could he do?

3. Sam took out his catch-all box and looked through all the bits and pieces. Just then his wife came by and asked, "What are you looking for?" "I don't know," replied Sam. "But I'll recognize it when I find it."

According to all rational ideas, you cannot look for things if you do not know what you are looking for, or know that you will recognize it when you find it. According to the laws of logic, that is impossible, but each and every one of you knows that it is possible. How? How can you look for something without knowing what you are looking for and still be sure you will recognize it?

Sam's goal to fix the vacuum cleaner was not easily understood in the sense that he knew exactly what he should do to make it work again. But Sam's understanding of how a vacuum cleaner works was so good that, with the help of his catch-all box, he could look for something that could make it work. Sam's goal had a clear Detector Function that helped him find a way.

The Detector Function generates meaning and content to things in life that would otherwise lack interest. The Detector Function often works so well that we talk about luck or divine intervention when it happens. Here is another example:

Joe borrowed a car from a good friend in New York. He picked the car up at an underground parking garage, but when he came up to the street he noticed that something was not working right. After a few blocks it became worse so he stopped and discovered that all four nuts on the right front wheel were loose. There were no tools in the car, so Joe tightened the nuts by hand, and then carefully drove on, trying to find a garage. After driving only 100 yards, a man walked across the street. Do you know what he had in his hand? Right you are. He was carrying a wrench. Joe borrowed it and tightened the nuts.

Was that luck? Was it divine intervention? Joe did not remember ever having seen a man with a wrench in his hand in Manhattan before. On the other hand, he had never had any reason to look for a way to tighten four wheel nuts before either.

The goal needs to be clear for the Detector Function to work well. You can influence this clarity yourself by defining, describing and trying to picture your goal as clearly as possible.

Everybody wants to live a good life. But what constitutes a good life? How would you answer that?

Ann is married and has two small children and a full-time job in a bank. We were introduced to her by someone who was very impressed with how much Ann could accomplish. In addition to her work and family, she was also actively involved in sports, and when the bank closed on Friday afternoon, she even had time for a half hour with her colleagues over a glass of wine. How did she manage?

When we talked to her about goals, Ann said she did not believe she had anything but a lot of half-goals. When we investigated her life more closely, we found she knew pretty well what she meant by a good life, at least now while her children were small. At a later stage the content may change, but for now it meant balancing the three elements that made up her life: family, work, and herself. She saw to it that she had sufficient time for herself so she did not get stuck in the "must-world," and during working hours she carried out her work with her job as the Detector. During her leisure time it was her family's needs that were the Detector.

Now let us look at common goals. In working life it is ultimately the responsibility of the boss to clarify goals. But it is not her or his responsibility alone. Everyone who contributes to a common goal can help make it clearer. One way of clarifying goals is to ask questions until you are convinced the goal is sufficiently clear.

"Sufficiently clear" means that the goal can be used to search for and find ways through. For instance, "the biggest possible profit" is not a clear goal. It is indistinct in regard to its content: Should it be viewed in the long or short term? It does not function as a Detector: How do you find ways to achieve the goal? A goal defined as increased market shares is much better. It is clearer in its content, and with a little thought can provide a Detector Function. You can also ask constructive questions that help you determine the content of the goal so it can function as a Detector.

Clarity in common goals depends to a large extent on

how freely you can talk about them, on what you have understood, how you have understood it – and above all on what you have not understood. Such talks can only take place in a working climate noted for a strong feeling of trust between bosses and associates, and between colleagues. Everyone involved needs to feel free to reveal to the others that they have not understood. Everyone needs to believe that it is alright to talk about what the goal means to them. It is not effective for different people in an organization to have different ideas about what the goal is, and that is what you get if you do not have trust.

When there is little or no trust, you play roles instead of behaving like yourself. You act the part of a boss instead of being one, you act the part of an interested salesman instead of really trying to understand what your customers need. You pretend to understand because you feel it is expected of you, instead of revealing that you have not yet understood, but that you really do want to comprehend.

In politics, where the party platform is often defined in such general terms that no one really knows what it means, the loyal party workers are actually destructive to the party when they simply accept the program instead of questioning it. But in order to question something, a trusting climate must exist so no one is regarded as disloyal if they ask questions.

So the first of the Generative Functions is the Detector. It generates meaning for things that would otherwise be meaningless. In order to develop strong Detector Functions in common goals, you must have a climate of trust so that everyone can communicate freely about the goal so that you create a clear picture of it.

THE GENERATOR FUNCTION. Attractive goals increase motivation, they create a stronger "will to." It is fairly easy to influence motivation with simple goals, for example in educating children and in advertising. There people try to link together an attractive "want" goal with the action the educator or salesman is aiming at. This is a very common way of looking at motivation. You do things not because you want the real end result of the action, but because you want the reward someone else is ready to give you if you act in the right way. This form of "motivation" is often more a case of manipulation; that is, tempting people to act against their true will by short-circuiting their understanding.

The basic, directly motivating value of goals naturally applies in all goal contexts. The goal has a Generator Function because it generates energy. In the case of more long term or complex goals, this means the goal and the picture of the goal create a constant flow of energy. If you work in a company that produces meaningful products or services, this can generate just such a constant flow of energy. Certain professions were previously regarded as "callings," the Church and medicine, for instance. To have a calling means to have a profession that in itself is so meaningful that it generates energy. Many people find sufficient motivation value in the fact that their goal is meaningful. Visionary leaders have worked with this motivation value throughout history because it continues to work as long as the vision is supported by actual experience.

A necessary condition for the goal to develop a Generator Function is that it must be your own, you need to "own" the goal before it can generate energy. This does not mean you have to own it 100%, but you need to feel you have influence over it.

Let us take an example. In hospitals, the goal of the organization is to give good service to patients. The administration in one hospital developed a pateint-service program that the nurses had to carry out as if they were robots. The nurses did not own the goal in that organization. However, the management in another hospital communicated "patient service" as a goal, and only specified the restrictions within which the patient-service program was to be carried out. The nurses themselves had to develop their own service program together with their patients. These nurses owned their goal.

So in order for other people's goals or company goals to be considered urgent and to generate energy, they must be in line with or go along with your own goals and values. All goals that are supposed to generate stimulation and energy must therefore be personally owned by each individual. In one company, they said, "The product is phenomenal. Everyone is proud to be a part of it. When a big order was shipped, everyone in the plant was taking pictures. There were ooh's and ah's, and people applauded. Can you believe it? For a computer?" We believe it. We can illustrate this kind of "owning" with the following story:

Walter is an engineer and an inventor. One fall he was going to take his rowboat up on land for the winter. His wife usually helped him, but that fall she was unavailable. In ancient Viking manner, Walter put a log under the boat's hull and started to pull it up. He soon found that if he made a groove around the log it was easier for the hull to roll on it, and he achieved two things. For one thing, the boat moved more steadily, and for another, the log moved further along the ground than along the hull of the boat so he did not have to move the log so often.

When Walter was finished with the job, he looked at his "invention" – and discovered that he had re-invented the wheel! Walter "owns" the wheel – all by himself he had worked his way clear to formulating the principle.

In a similar way, you can own your goals if you are allowed to create your own understanding of what the goal means. The wheel is owned by many people, but that does not matter. The important thing for Walter is that <u>he</u> owns it.

You should own your goals, but that is not enough. Your goals should also be a challenge if you want them to generate energy. What is a challenge to one person may be frightening to another, and dull to a third. Whether a goal presents a challenge is entirely an individual question. One person may feel challenged when s/he has a time limit, another when s/he is faced with a difficult construction problem, a third when s/he is trying to resolve a conflict, and a fourth by something else. Mary felt the challenge in becoming a more and more competent violinist, and Sam wanted to find the solution to his vacuum cleaner problem.

If you want the people in your organization to believe that they are allowed to develop their own goals, you must first create a climate of respect for their right to have their own opinions.

The need to please, and other expressions of role playing instead of authentic behavior, is strengthened in those organizations that have a climate that stresses conformity. You will not find much respect for the individual's own opinion in such organizations. Instead, "the principle of good personal relationships" seems to be the guiding norm for cooperation.

"The principle of good personal relationships" means that you should live up to other people's expectations and avoid creating conflicts that might upset their plans. In such a climate, there are few possibilities for using the contributions from the person whose work has other demands on the challenge than those laid down by convention. Put together, these contributions could mean development towards a common goal, but "the principle of good personal relationships" prevents it.

To make the boss' goal your own without first finding out to what extent it coincides with your own goal may feel motivating in the short term. In the long term, however, you do not gain anything in the form of stimulation, flow of energy or creativity. In the short term, such goals function as "carrots," motivating pseudo-goals. You do things to get the reward, not because you want to attain the Result Value.

So the second of the Generative Functions is the Generator. It generates energy if you feel that you own the goal and find it challenging. Only the individual can decide for herself or himself whether the goal is challenging. So in order to develop the Generator Function, the climate must permit respect for every individual's own experience and opinions.

The Detector and the Generator Must Work Together. When the Detector works, then you know how to act. But that does not help very much if you do not have enough energy to act with. Of course you know how to fill in an expense account form, but not right now...

On the other hand, if the Generator works, but not the Detector, then you have the energy but do not know what to do with it. In its extreme form, this causes frustration or panic. Some organizations seem to believe in activity for its own sake: "Don't just stand there – do something!" Companies like this usually have a lot of "fast but wrong" managers and subordinates. In other organizations that value results more than activity as such, they know they need to find the Detector before they can act: "Don't just do something – stand it!"

We want to stress that the Detector Function and the Generator Function must cooperate if you want to reach your goals.

THE DEVELOPMENT FUNCTION. The goal's third Generative Function is to create a basis for Development. By Development we mean an intentional change in direction toward a definite goal. Change without goals can be wobbly or easy-going, and as sometimes seen as an expression of flexibility. We have nothing against flexibility as long as it is not used as a euphemism for an inability to let things alone, for changing things just for the sake of change.

Healthy people need development. You need to stretch toward goals and extend the boundaries of your previous experience. If this need is not satisfied, disruptions occur. Several of the dysfunctions in modern society are a result either of people being prevented from seeking development, or of not understanding that they need development. Vandalism, drug-abuse and different forms of senseless crime and violence are manifestations of such disruptions or dysfunctions.

Who am I? What is my identity? As we said in the introduction, there are two answers to this question:

1. I am a product of my history; I define myself by reasons, by where I came from. This is "reason identity."

2. I identify myself with where I am going. What is specific to me is not my history, but the future I want to create. This is "will identity."

"Will identity" is the basis for Development. To have the courage to develop by stretching the boundaries of your previous experience, you need self-esteem, what Abraham Maslow defined as "an expectation of success." We used Maslow's definition of self-esteem as the basis for our own definition of success: "to reach goals." You expect success because you have had success. "Success breeds success." The core of what we call motivation is a striving toward a greater self-esteem, a striving toward a better ability to take care of things and solve problems yourself. For this to happen you need to succeed, you need to reach your goals. And to do that, your goals must be realistic. This requirement, that your goals must be realistic, can be fulfilled if you are completely objective when you set them. "Realistic" goals does not mean they have to be easy to reach. They certainly would not be much of a challenge then. Realistic means the goals should be possible to reach.

To make an organization's goals – the common goals – realistic, they should be tested in a climate of objectivity and honesty. Objectivity means having a constructively critical attitude, demanding consistency between different actions, being open to questions, and having the courage to accept the consequences if you are wrong.

TO SUMMARIZE.

The Detector, Generator and Development Functions together create the basic Motivating Values: Meaning, Energy and Self-Esteem. These Development Values are associated to such a high degree with true human values that we could just as easily have chosen to call them existential values or humanistic values.

To generate these values, a goal must be Clear, Challenging and Realistic. Regarding individual goals (and all goals must be more or less individual because you need to "own" them), you can influence your motivation by clarifying your goals and making sure they are challenging and realistic.

Figure 2 illustrates what our model looks like now. We have included the new terms used in the latter part of this chapter.

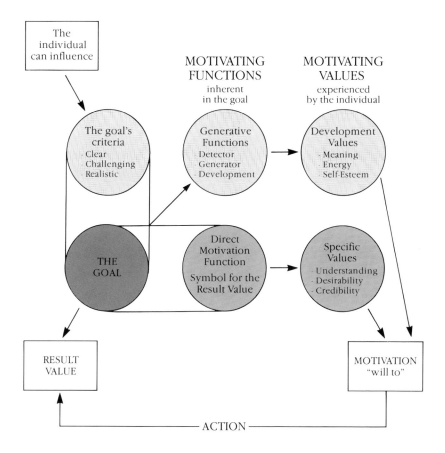

FIGURE 2

Finally, we have said something about the climate within an organization necessary for these relationships to work so that different staff members, each from their own initial position and goal, can strive towards the goals that are common for the entire organization. Everyone needs to feel that s/he can influence her or his own goals so s/he can take responsibility for the common goals.

If you look at goals in such a broad sense as we have done here, the total concept and theory is so complicated that most people cannot remember it, even if they followed the discussion. But you do not need to be able to describe the theory of goal orientation. What you should remember is that you should demand from all your goals that they be Clear, Challenging and Realistic, and that there be a correlation between the effectiveness and long-range profitability in an organization and a social climate where Trust, Respect for the individual and Objectivity can be found.

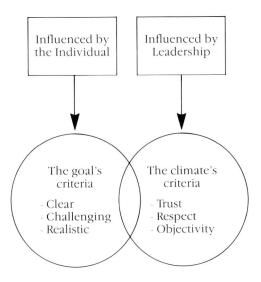

FIGURE 3

— 68 —

CHAPTER 6

GOAL CONFLICTS AND GOALS IN WIDER PERSPECTIVE

PRIORITIES.

You may often have several goals at the same time. If they are not directly contradictory to each other, they can still be in conflict because they compete for the same assets – your time and energy, for example. You cannot concentrate your attention on both work and family at the same time, on both immediate, short-term goals and on long-term goals.

As a leader, you probably find it difficult to become involved in your subordinates' development and your other business responsibilities at the same time. The most usual solution to this problem is to let your emotional impulses guide your choice of goal. You set priorities based on what "feels" most important. But what feels most important is often whatever will most quickly lead to your "feeling good." It feels important to free yourself from tension in a conflict situation.

Sometimes you have two goals; one that is not clear and one that is. In deciding between them, you probably most often choose the one that is most distinct, not because it is the most important, but simply because it is the easiest one to see.

The clearest goals often feel most important. We said earlier that goals should be clear. But we do not mean that clear goals are more important than those that are less clear. One woman told us she assigned priorities according to the maximal-acoustic principle: "He who shouts loudest, gets helped first." It is a principle, but not an effective one.

One man complained that he never had enough time, that he missed certain jobs and that he often came late to meetings. "But," he bragged, "I travel by plane at least 40 times a year and I've never missed a flight." From our perspective, he automatically gave such goals priority because they were so clear.

Giving priority to whatever can be seen, felt and heard most often leads to self-sabotage. You are not anywhere near as effective as you could be or as you believe you are. You may sometimes rationalize your actions; that is, look for rational explanations for actions that were largely based on emotions. Of course you are allowed to have emotional needs, and even to let these important needs guide your actions. But you should refrain from hiding your true motives behind a veil of false reason. You should refrain from it because it is harmful to both your own mental condition and to the climate in your organization.

We have previously shown that you can gain access to several alternative actions by getting distance. In a similar way, you can learn to see goals and goal conflicts in a wider perspective. If you are working on a clearly defined job that you know how to do, and you are not subjected to disturbances, then you should not have any problem with priorities. Even if you plan to develop this single job into a whole project – an activity with an objective that has defined limits both in problem areas and time – you still should not have any problems setting priorities. You solve the problems that come up in relation to the project's goal, you have a focus.

As a project leader you have the project's goal and structure to help you set priorities. But it immediately becomes more difficult when you have to run several projects in parallel, or when development work has to be done in tandem with your normal workload. That is when you probably lack a common focus for the different jobs.

Our general recommendation to help you achieve an overview and get distance is that you should try to see your work as a whole. When you are hired for a job, you are usually given a position, not a goal. Even if there is a description of the work involved, it is seldom formulated so the job can be seen as a whole, with a number of connected tasks. However, there is nothing to prevent you from looking at your work as a whole, as a super-project.

"What is the primary result I want to achieve?" If you ask yourself this, you can limit goals and work areas, you can set time limits and see yourself as a project leader, which of course you are – it is all about your own job. This does not mean that you ignore certain jobs, but you gain a rational basis for deciding which order to put them in.

The most important thing after that is to get the super-project's Detector Function working. Then you can sort out those mini-goals that will best help you realize the super-project's goal. If you have a clear picture of what your areas of responsibility are, and what it means to achieve good results and smooth cooperation, then you have a good background picture for your super-project.

By a good picture we mean a clear idea or image of what needs to be done and how. It is more a question of following certain patterns that you feel at home with than of following fixed programs.

Let us try to illustrate these ideas with the help of Ann, the bank employee we talked about in Chapter 5. There were three elements in her picture of "a good life": a good family life, a good work life, and physical well-being. It would seem reasonable that she sees her private life and work life as two super-projects. Both projects are there all the time, but depending on whether it is work time or free time, she handles the problems that crop up in different ways.

In her leisure time, it is her family that is in focus. Her idea of what constitutes "a good life," at least in this phase of her family life, functions as her primary goal. While her children are small, Ann's definition of "a good life" is to have a lot of contact with them, so needlework, socializing with her friends, going to the movies and reading are all secondary activities on her list of priorities. When the children are older, her requirements will be different and she can change her super-project's goals.

Ann's executive position in the bank is very demanding. It is obvious that now and then she has to take her work home with her, or that she must put in a few hours' work over weekends. However, she looks for a solution to this problem with the help of her private life super-project. Ann's work is her other super-project. She asks herself what her primary jobs are, then deals with the problems that come up in relation to them. Of course sometimes the children are sick and she has no alternative but to stay home herself. But first she always tries to find solutions that will make it possible for her to do her job during actual office hours.

Ann's husband seems to have a similar attitude to his life. He also has an executive position in his company and when there is a conflict between his work and his family life, he and Ann work together to find the best solution for the whole. During office hours, Ann concentrates on job priorities, but still gives consideration to her family. During her leisure time, the family has priority, but she still considers her job, her husband's work situation, and her own personal needs. That is a dynamic view of life. There are always desired results and desired limits that you strive to reach and maintain. But it is possible to adjust and adapt these by considering the whole picture just for the time being.

A super-project can be likened to a tapestry; it is an interweaving of cooperation between you and your associates and superiors. Each person is responsible for part of the pattern and chooses the steps best suited to mesh her or his part with the overall design. In a similar way, Ann and her husband create their tapestry by interweaving two professions, a common family life and two individuals' desire for physical well-being.

Some elements in a tapestry are sharply outlined against this background of flowing and intertwining patterns, others are in a softer focus. Some elements appear only once, others are repeated. How do they fit into the overall pattern? If they fit in, they can become new mini-projects that must be coordinated with what is already under way. If they do not fit in, should you then try to get rid of them or put them on ice until the time is ripe? That is what Ann did with needlework, friends and going to the movies. They do not fit into her overall pattern just now.

Time and time structures are important for limiting all projects, including super-projects. Without the structures, the goal is indistinct and the Detector Function is weak. But with clear time structures, it is easier to set priorities among different alternatives.

OPPOSITION TO GOALS.

Most people agree that organizations need goals. It is the common goals that are the really uniting elements in any organization. Earlier we mentioned that the true identity of a person is expressed by her or his goals and intentions. There is a parallel to that for organizations: If you have common goals then you also have a common identity, which gives you a good basis for solidarity within your organization.

Goals give you a basis for dealing with conflicts and common ideas that contributes to finding ways through more easily. When we talk about goals for an organization, we mean something other than precise wordings such as "highest possible profit," or verbose visions of how the Utopian state is to be realized. Goals need to be understood in the same way by everyone, and they need to be desirable and realistic. Later we will come back to how organizations' goals can be active aids to unite people and to find a direction. Most people agree that organizations need goals. But when it comes to themselves, their attitude is often quite different.

In our "Life and Career Program," when we try to interest people in setting goals for themselves, it is no longer so obvious to them that they should have goals. Many people resist deciding on their goals. There are several explanations for that. We have already identified two of them; namely, that with clear goals, the risk of failure and the conflicts between yourself and the people around you become more apparent. But there are other explanations as well.

As soon as you begin to think about long-term or overlapping goals, uncertainty increases. Some people are thrown off by what they feel is too deep or highbrow in life goals and career goals. Others are repelled by an attitude that they regard as too rational and coldly analytical. One recurring objection is: "If I have a clear goal, there is a risk that I will confine myself to it so exclusively that I will not allow myself to see other opportunities that turn up along the way." This objection is based on the idea that goals confine you, which we, naturally, do not agree with.

Behind these objections lie a couple of general resistances: in part the fear of failure, which we covered earlier, and in part the fear of becoming confined, the fear that you will lose your freedom. Resistance comes from the same motive as the negative reflexes in the "must-world."

To avoid failure was the motive for an escape-reflex, and to avoid being invaded was the motive for a no-reflex.

The goals you choose yourself that fulfill the basic criteria have exactly the opposite effect. They are a requirement for success. Fear of failure stunts your possibilities to develop, and is one of the more important forms of self-sabotage. If you refrain from setting goals because you are afraid of missing opportunities, then you have completely misunderstood how goals function. The Detector helps you find several possibilities, it expands the structure – not the other way around. The goal's clarity and desirability help you both to keep on track toward success and to hang on until you get there. Clear goals simplify your decisions. You do not need to waste energy on carefully weighing up each small detail. Clear goals help you sort out your options.

But they also help you become aware of possibilities that you otherwise would not have seen. These new possibilities can be so interesting that they give you reason to revise your goals, to choose another direction. A clear idea of what your goals are gives you the opportunity to be dynamic, to take a roundabout way or to momentarily stray off on a sidetrack without getting lost. Look at water as a parallel. Water does not know how to make its way, but it knows where it should go – downwards. When water comes to a depression, it cannot run downwards anymore. So it evaporates and moves on with the wind until it can continue its way down again as rain.

To have a good time intentionally during an examination, or to enjoy a family weekend during the final stages of a negotiation project is not self-sabotage. By this we mean that a goal gives you freedom. With the help of a goal you can evaluate different alternatives in relation to each other, including the possibilities you do not want to miss. And in a completely irrational way, a goal even gives you the freedom to just do nothing once in a while, simply because you want to.

Your goals are the integrating elements in your personality. They unite your actions and attitudes, your search for knowledge, your desires and beliefs. They define your will-identity. The better united the different parts are, the more consistent they are with each other, then the more well-integrated and healthy you are as a personality.

Jung said that people can only be fully understood in relation to their goals. The clearer your goals are, the more understandable you become both to yourself and to others. You become understandable, not in a static way such as 2+2=4, but as dynamically understandable as truth, happiness, solidarity and trust. These are terms everyone is familiar with, but they are always just as fresh and positively surprising each time you encounter them.

ORGANIZATION IDENTITY.

Companies have identities as well as people. Companies with well-integrated goals and values work well, they are healthy. Their identities work like Detectors that are everywhere at once, which helps employees choose the right actions.

Company identity is the core of what is usually called the organization's culture: a collection of values or expressions of will that are mutually supportive to each other. In recent years, we have directed our attention to an increasing degree to the connection between companies' cultures and their successes. There are countless research results that indicate that successful companies are so thanks to their strong and uniting cultures.

The best-known example in this case is IBM. The company's strong policy toward customers' needs, and in particular the customers' service needs, is summarized in a kind of core-evaluation or company identity: "IBM means service."

"IBM means service" is something more than just an advertising slogan. It is a term for a lifestyle, for a business policy found throughout daily work. Identity differs from a slogan because it is integrated into daily business. Or as Deal & Kennedy say: "What makes them more than slogans is the degree to which these phrases capture something people in the organization deeply believe in. These words take on rich and concrete meaning." (T. E. Deal & A. A. Kennedy, Corporate Cultures, Addison-Wesley, 1982).

The difference between a slogan and an identity can be illustrated like this. Many companies say "Our personnel is our most important asset." Some companies treat their people as if they believed in that saying, so for them it is an identity. Other companies say it because it sounds nice and progressive – for them it is a slogan.

Identity is made up of several mutually supportive evaluations. IBM's evaluation, "respect for the individual," is a living reality in the organization. "Respect for the individual" supports the evaluation "IBM means service" in the following way:

Respect for the individual exists in many different forms. IBM's "open-door policy" is one demonstration of respect for the individual. It means that every member of the working staff has the right to contact her or his boss' boss if s/he has a complaint or other comment to make. One aim of this is to make superiors open to their fellow workers' opinions. They should really listen and care about what their fellow workers think. If you are open to your fellow workers' opinions, you learn to be open to other people's opinions too. Customers are also people with opinions, and it is important that everyone understand that if they want to live up to "IBM means service."

A company's identity is a continuing goal over the years. It is an expression of the values you want to express in your daily work. But companies also need to reach other long-term goals that are challenging and that can generate energy in the organization. We call such goals <u>Strategic Visions</u>.

In his book <u>Megatrends</u>, John Naisbitt gives an excellent example of Strategic Vision; namely, President John F. Kennedy's order to NASA at the beginning of the 1960s: "Before the end of this decade, we shall put a man on the moon." Such goals have a very impressive motivation effect.

We have taken a sidestep from our subject, Personal Effectiveness, in order to show parallels between an individual's and an organization's identity. Strategic Vision in companies also has its counterpart among individuals. We call it Destination.

DEVELOPMENT GOALS – DESTINATION.

We agree with the idea that development is a fundamental human need. You need to extend your boundaries, to grow and move into new phases. In a way similar to companies' strategic visions, goals connected with your search for these new development phases can generate powerful amounts of energy. We call such individual development goals Destination.

Destination should fulfill the same requirements as all your other goals; that is, it should be Clear, Challenging and Realistic. Otherwise it cannot work well, otherwise it cannot generate Meaning, Energy and Self-Esteem. Destination is something new to try your strength against. It is in Destination's nature to be challenging, and that is its most important purpose – to increase your vitality and stimulate you during the workday.

If Destination lies very much off course from your other goals, there is a risk that it will lead to discord, just as with other goal conflicts. You may recognize this from you own life, or from someone else who, at some point in their life, decided to do something radically different from what they had done before.

However, Destination can act as a tremendous source of energy, even in your daily work, if it is in line with what you have done so far. If you choose a deviating Destination, you will probably derive less benefit from this energy source in your present workday.

Promotion can be a Destination in business, but it does not have to be. A higher position is not necessarily the same thing as Development by our definition. The prestige of the new position and your desire to live up to the demands of the people around you to be good may outweigh your desire for personal development. You need to doublecheck your goals sometimes, to look at them critically and actively both from an overall perspective and in relation to your actual situation. Your external situation changes as you become older, the children grow up, etc. So even if no specific event occurs, your situation still changes. You need to know – and then stop and think about – what Development means to you now and in the future. You need to periodically review your goals and your Destination.

You can live in a continuous state of Development once you become aware that the possibility exists. Periods of immobility can be painful. You can find the parts of life where there is no development less attractive in comparison with the parts where you feel you can develop. The relationship between a married couple can stagnate just as much as development at work can come to a halt. If one part of your life is stagnating, you may focus on another, more stimulating part as compensation. The workaholic escapes from an unhappy home, and the hypochondriac with a fixation on leisure time takes every opportunity to keep away from his job. But if you are aware that you have access to development in far more situations than you might see at first glance, you can change you condition.

Development, just like challenge, is intimately linked with personal and individual attitudes. They are different for each person, but they also change during different periods in the same person's life. In one phase, promotion can mean development because it brings opportunities for greater responsibility. In another phase, further development within the structure of the present position might be preferable.

For instance, some positions call for solitary, specialist abilities, such as designers, accountants and systems analysts. On the other hand, to be a leader means to manage and cooperate with other people. If you are promoted from a specialist to a leadership position, you must choose whether you want to continue working alone, and possibly be in competition with your staff, or if you want to cooperate with them – or if you do not really want the promotion at all.

Development is not confined to a time, place or position. You may find your greatest development opportunities within the structure of your present position.